SO[illegible]H AND THE LUNAR BLADES

J W B Rowley

Sock Sloth and the Lunar Blades

Printed in the United Kingdom

Published by Rainbow House Publishing
85 Great Portland Street
London
W1W 7LT

www.rainbowhousepublishing.com

Identifiers:

ISBN: 978-1-0686912-0-1 (paperback)
ISBN: 978-1-0686912-1-8 (e-book)

Available in paperback and e-book.

CONTENTS

Chapter 1: An Important Mission. 1

Chapter 2: A Terrible Trip 6

Chapter 3: The Legend of the Lunar King 8

Chapter 4: The Chillbone Maze 10

Chapter 5: Into the Depths 14

Chapter 6: Machine Madness 18

Chapter 7: Cinema Catastrophe 21

Chapter 8: The Solar Eclipse 24

Chapter 9: Grandpa Panda to the Rescue 26

Chapter 10: Wacky's Wrath 30

Chapter 11: Rocket Pig Grenade. 34

Chapter 12: A Watery Surprise 37

Chapter 13: The Return of the Lunar King. 40

About the Author. 43

CHAPTER 1

AN IMPORTANT MISSION

Sock Sloth woke up one morning to find the world upside down.

And indeed, it was, from his perspective.

He was hanging on a branch which stretched horizontally from one wall to the other of his office in downtown Aridonia.

He immediately realised that he was the one upside down, not the entire world.

Sock Sloth slowly climbed down from the branch and onto his office chair.

You see, Sock Sloth had always felt he was a bit different to everyone else. And the thing that made him different was not his superspeed or climbing skills. Well, maybe you could argue that his superspeed as a sloth made him different, but the real thing that made everyone stop and stare was his pair of stripy red and white socks. And it was these socks that had helped him to get to where he was in life.

Together with his best friend Rick the Panda aka Sir Bamboo (on account of the amount of bamboo he consumes), Sock Sloth was the proud co-owner of the Super Awesome Dudes Crime Fighting Agency or SAD for short.

That September morning, whilst the sun was still rising in the sky, the office telephone burst into life and almost exploded with the force of its ringing.

Rick shuffled over to where it was, muttering what sounded like 'haven't even had breakfast yet.'

On picking up the receiver, he heard a flurry of rushed, shrill words on the other end. "Come! Please help! The Lunar Blades have been stolen!" In his morning drowsy state, still dreaming of lush green shoots of bamboo, Rick responded, "The Bamboo Blades? Oh goodie!" Furiously though he was interrupted, "No! The Lunar Blades L-U-N-A-R B-L-A-D-E-S!"

"Ah, ok, I get it now," Rick reassured the caller.

"They've been stolen," continued the agitated female voice at the end of the line, "by Wacky Bottomsmirk and you just have to get them back. Please help me!"

"And you are?" Rick asked.

But before the voice could respond, the telephone line fell silent once more.

Sock Sloth peered inquisitively at Rick from behind his huge desk made from an ageing tree trunk.

"What was that all about?"

Rick replied – "The Lunar Blades have been stolen!"

Sock Sloth's eyes widened in shock as Rick continued "by Wacky Bottomsmirk."

There was a moment's silence before Sock Sloth, looking bedazzled, asked "Really?"

"Yep," confirmed Rick, sidling up to a fresh green shoot of bamboo.

"Are you sure?" Sock Sloth asked him.

"Yep! That's what she said on the phone."

"Who was it that called?" Sock Sloth questioned.

"Dunno!" Rick responded – his attention now firmly set on stripping the leaves from the bamboo stem in front of him.

"Then let's go and find out then!" Sock Sloth declared.

Rick had known Sock Sloth for long enough to know that this bamboo stem was likely to be his last for a while, as once his friend was on a mission it was hard to stop him, let alone catch up with him.

"Ok Rick, gather together everything you need..." Sock Sloth began before chastising him...

"No, you don't need those extra additional twelve sacks of bamboo, no, no, no Rick for goodness' sake – we're meant to be part of a dynamic crime fighting agency – they will only slow us down."

"Fine," retorted Rick, "then I shall bring my ultimate secret agent rucksack, which is totally not filled to the brim with bamboo, a pair of scissors, masking tape, and a length of super strength rope. But mainly bamboo!"

"Ok, ok," despaired Sock Sloth – "You win! Now let's get going."

"So, who is Whacky Bottomburp?" asked Rick, puzzled by what they were about to walk into.

"He's an evil tyrant of the worst kind, with an army of iguanas who do his bidding. And he's also a formidable walrus!" Sock Sloth confirmed.

"If he's a walrus, how can he stay only on land – doesn't he also need to be near water too?" Rick asked sensibly.

"He has, what's known as a cybernetic bodysuit. And also his name is Bottomsmirk not Bottomburp just for the record." Sock Sloth confirmed.

"Who was that lady on the phone then?" Rick said, "She sounded very distressed."

"Well, my guess is that she's the immortal blade keeper, whose sole duty is to keep those blades safe." Sock Sloth deduced.

"Well, when she spoke, there were mentions of iguanas in tanks," Rick suddenly recalled, his memory improving with every bite of bamboo.

"Blimey!" exclaimed Sock Sloth. "We'd better hurry."

As his tummy flipped a somersault – something told him they were about to embark on a very dangerous mission indeed.

CHAPTER 2
A TERRIBLE TRIP

Aridonia, where Sock Sloth and Rick the Panda lived, was a large city, inhabited by over thirteen million people.

On all sides, they were surrounded by harsh, sandy deserts.

In the middle of the largest desert stood the imposing Mount Mammoth.

The Chillbone Maze, home to the Lunar Blades, stood proudly, perched eight-thousand metres at the top. It was almost as tall as Everest!

"I'm bored! Can we have lunch?" asked Rick hopefully, but only ten minutes into their journey.

"No, we've only just started - and we haven't even left the city yet!" Sock Sloth chastised.

They went left. They went right. They even at one point went backwards after Rick mistakenly left his back-pack at a bus stop.

Until finally, they reached the outskirts of the city, both of them feeling much grumpier and more discombobu-lated than when they first embarked on their adventure.

Rick, chewing on a bamboo leaf turned to Sock Sloth and asked, "Socky, why do you think Wacky has stolen the Lunar Blades now?"

It was a good question and one that Sock Sloth had to think long and hard about before the answer dawned on him.

"The solar eclipse is meant to be happening soon. And that is when the Lunar Blades are at their strongest." Sock Sloth looked more determined than ever.

"That is what Whacky was planning – to use them when they're at their most powerful. It's very worrying indeed."

Turning to Rick he encouraged – "Come on Rick, we have to get there and fast. The damage the blades can do could be unimaginable."

CHAPTER 3

THE LEGEND OF THE LUNAR KING

Once, in the desert land of Aridonia, sat a lofty mountain full of the most beautiful colourful plants, trees and flowers scattered all over grassland that grew on all sides. This soon became known as the Lost Grassland. This grassland was also home to the Gallery of the Mystics, which also happened to be home to the Lunar King, the Lord of Lightning.

But with its serene beauty and natural riches, it fell victim to an ambitious, evil king, who wanted the mountain and its grasslands for himself. One day in a bold move, the Demon King's Army attacked the mountain, making sure all the inhabitants fled like screaming goats.

The Lunar King, not wanting the Demon King to win, was left with no choice but to transform the grassland into arid deserts as far as the eye could see. Fires started, trees burnt down, flowers died, and the temple at the heart of the Gallery of the Mystics was destroyed.

Not wanting the land as it had become, the Demon King retreated, and the Lunar King lived out his days surrounded by the arid climate that he had created.

Many years later, as the Lunar King was nearing his end, he knew that somehow, he had to get rid of his powers. So, he used the remnants of the temple to create The Chillbone Maze. Worried about further attacks from enemies, he filled it with death-defying traps.

Then he poured all his powers into two large katanas (large Japanese swords). As he did so, he instructed his only daughter, Tibono, to guard the blades forever. In doing so, he blessed her with immortality before he passed away to another realm. His body was buried in the centre of the mountain, never to be seen again.

CHAPTER 4

THE CHILLBONE MAZE

Staring up at the imposing mass of Mount Mammoth, Sock Sloth knew there was no alternative. They had to get help if they were to scale the eight-thousand metre vertical climb that lay ahead of them. Rick was certainly in no condition to scale anything bigger than a tree, and with time not on their side, there was only one thing for it.

It had to be Grandpa Panda to the rescue.

Thankfully, Grandpa Panda had been in the military all his life and was able to call in a favour from his former army buddies.

One quick call from Sock Sloth, and the promise of being paid in lots of bamboo, and Grandpa Panda touched down on the outskirts of the city in a helicopter armed with everything the boys needed to complete their quest.

The flight was seamless, which was much more than could be said for Rick's tummy, which rumbled throughout.

When they touched down at the maze – and waved farewell to Grandpa Panda – it was quite a sight to see.

Fifteen-metre-high stone walls surrounded them. Overgrown vines were tangled in and out of broken brick-work and large chunks of stone were falling to the ground.

That must have been where the army of iguanas had forced their way in whilst driving their tanks.

At the entrance to the maze stood a tall, imposing woman, whose shadow towered over them. Her face was mostly hidden by a long, black cloak with intriguing silver markings. But from what Sock Sloth could make out – she had jet black hair, a long nose and the darkest of eyes, distrustful of anyone.

In his mind, Sock Sloth knew this had to be Tibono, the immortal blade keeper.

He made note of the fact she was holding a spear with a ruby red crystal spike on top of it.

"That must be the Spear of Destiny," Sock Sloth signalled to Rick – "It shoots fire as a deterrent to those who try to enter the maze."

Rick looked startled at the prospect of anything able to shoot fire.

As they edged closer, the cloaked blade-keeper began to speak to them in a deep, trembling voice.

"Welcome to the Chillbone Maze! And thank you for coming so quickly."

Sock Sloth and Rick exchanged knowing looks before the woman continued.

"This is a place where many have perished. I trust that you have brought everything necessary with you as once you enter there is no turning back."

They both nodded in agreement, but Sock Sloth stopped her from going further by adding, "Please tell us again what exactly happened here last night?"

"They approached just after midnight." Tibono began hesitantly.

"At first it was just two iguanas on foot, having an argument. Then when I was distracted, two tanks emerged, firing acid bombs that burnt my skin to the bone. They fired at me, hitting me on my foot and I dropped my spear, which became covered in all the rubble. I had no choice but to move aside as I was in so much pain writhing on the floor from their attack. It took me hours to recover the spear, and when I did, the Lunar Blades had already been taken. That's when I called you."

On saying this, she lifted the hem of her cloak to reveal a red, shrivelled leg before continuing,

"I will recover but I'll always be left with the scarring. Sometimes this job is such a burden."

Sock Sloth felt sorry for her. It hadn't been her choice to guard the maze or become immortal – it was her late father's request and she'd gone along with it out of loyalty to him. He wondered at what price.

Rick looked at Sock Sloth and Sock Sloth returned a concerned look back at Rick.

"Erm how long will it take to get to the centre of the maze where the Lunar Blades were kept?" Rick asked, his tummy gurgling. He was much happier when they were back at the office as he could eat all the bamboo from the cupboards he wanted.

Sock Sloth adjusted his red and white socks so they were pulled up as high as they would go.

"You can take all the time you need," he smiled at Rick, "but I'm going into superspeed mode" and with that, he disappeared inside, calling back to his panda pal, "I'll see you in there."

Rick shrugged his enormous black and white shoulders, and followed at a much slower pace, worried now that they wouldn't be back out of the maze in time for dinner.

CHAPTER 5
INTO THE DEPTHS

Once Sock Sloth was alone, despite being super speedy, he wondered how dangerous the maze would be. But his question was soon answered when fifteen flaming arrows shot straight past his head!

He realised in his haste he had stood on a well-camouflaged stone pressure plate.

Well, this is going to be fun he thought sarcastically to himself.

But every single challenge he faced was no match for his super speed.

Every time the maze threw a conundrum at him, he whizzed past it all. Until that is, he reached the super duper ultimate tricky test sheet.

Speedy he may have been on foot but speedy in Maths, not so much.

It took him a while to work out the answer to one plus one. But when he finally realised that the answer was two, he was transported to the centre of the maze by what could only be described as an underfoot conveyer belt, that moved extremely fast.

His thoughts went to Rick – and he wondered how his friend would be getting on with all the challenges the maze had to offer.

But as he arrived, he spotted a large cage being pushed along on wheels by two iguanas. It contained a massive ball of black and white fur. Cast away on a nearby podium sat Rick's backpack, filled to the brim with bamboo.

Sock Sloth ducked under a nearby vine so he couldn't be seen, his heart pounding out of concern for his best friend.

How had they managed to get to Rick so quickly? He'd used his superspeed and had been sure that Rick would have been much further behind him.

Perhaps the iguanas knew of a short cut?

But as he pondered this and many other questions, Sock Sloth came up with a cunning plan.

And he was always very determined about his plans.

This one involved saving Rick and the Lunar Blades at the same time.

Meanwhile, Wacky Bottomsmirk was in the corner observing Rick, but unaware that he was being observed by Sock Sloth.

"Hmmm, take him away!" he ordered maniacally to the iguanas who obeyed without question or even lifting their drooped heads.

Sly as a snake, Sock Sloth ran to Rick's backpack, grabbing a bamboo shoot and threw it at Wacky, before promptly disappearing again.

"What's this?" Whacky looked around him, and then at the offending piece of bamboo. He sniffed it, before tossing it to the ground once more. "Will someone please bin this useless bit of bamboo?" he cackled.

But from the cage a mighty eruption took everyone, except Sock Sloth, by surprise.

"Bin bamboo?" The towering bulk of Rick the Panda came to life.

"BIN BAMBOO?" he roared, a demonic flare erupting inside of him as he tore apart the iron bars of his cage one by one, leaving the nearby iguanas to screech and disperse as fast as they could.

At first, Whacky looked bemused. What had he said that was so bad?

But he soon felt the full force of Rick's 150-kilogram weight descending on him.

Rick then contentedly grabbed the discarded bamboo shoot, his full weight on top of Whacky – and began to chew in a much more measured way.

"I think you just broke my back!" Whacky wailed in agony.

"Never, ever bin any bamboo!" Rick retorted.

Sock Sloth was the only one not surprised by Rick's reaction but as he emerged from his hiding place, delighted in saying,

"Whacky Bottomsmirk, you're going to prison for orchestrating and stealing the Lunar Blades!"

CHAPTER 6
MACHINE MADNESS

Everything moved very fast after that. Wacky was airlifted to downtown Aridonia, where he was sentenced to life in prison.

Sock Sloth and Rick were hailed as heroes and amid all the back slapping and congratulations one small detail had been missed.

And that something was troubling Sock Sloth. Surely that had been too easy.

"Was it too easy?" Sock Sloth asked Rick, who was now contentedly tearing leaves off a new bamboo shoot.

"Yeah, you're right." Rick whispered back. "You always are."

Meanwhile as Whacky was beginning his prison sentence – something completely different was going on in his cell.

Sock Sloth gasped, as he realised what that small but significant detail was. They may have captured Whacky but what about the Lunar Blades themselves? Where were they?

The thing they hadn't realised is that Whacky still had them on him – they had gone undetected as he was still wearing his cybernetic suit. During his capture and whilst Rick had been squashing him with his bulk, Wacky had made them invisible.

Now, having taken them out of his suit, he was able to cut through the titanium prison bars, slay multiple robot guards, before rounding on the large mechanical dragon that was the ultimate defense against any escape plan.

The dragon leapt up to stop Whacky from passing. It fired multiple missiles in his direction. Whacky deftly deflected each and every one, using the almighty power of the Lunar Blades. Plasma rays followed. Again, the blades helped him to be so agile, despite his Walrus bulk, that he could skirt around everyone. The dragon reared up onto his hind legs and used its ultimate weapon, the lightning blaster.

It proved to be an extremely long fight. In fact, it was so long, you could have easily eaten a Christmas dinner whilst watching – pigs in blankets and all, and even have had time for dessert.

But in the end, the power of the Lunar Blades proved too much for the mechanical dragon. The Lunar King's powers had all been stored in those two powerful katanas and as the Lord of Lightning – there was never really going to be another match.

The city of Aridonia was once again in mortal danger as Whacky Bottomsmirk wielded the Lunar Blades – it was a terrifying reality that only a few were currently aware of.

CHAPTER 7

CINEMA CATASTROPHE

Meanwhile in another part of the city, Sock Sloth and Rick the Panda were enjoying ice cream as part of a celebratory trip to the cinema, complete with jelly sweets, a hot dog and in Rick's case more bamboo from his now recovered backpack.

Before the film started and whilst the adverts were rolling, they began whispering about the Lunar Blades and where Whacky could have stashed them.

"Why do I feel like everything with Whacky is far from over?" Sock Sloth began, a sense of unease rising in his throat. He uncharacteristically scratched his socks.

"Dunno," answered Rick nonchalantly.

"Dunno!" repeated Sock Sloth

Yes, "Dunno, dunno, dunno," repeated Rick comically thinking of a detective cartoon he'd once seen featuring a lithe pink cat.

"You know if he does still have the Lunar Blades, then that means he can still cause all manner of mayhem and destruction?" Sock Sloth was suddenly nervous.

"You mean he could bin more bamboo?" Rick's expression had quickly turned from one of laughter to that same demonic flare that had woken inside him at The Chillbone Maze.

Sock Sloth had never seen his friend move so fast for pandas are not known for their speed, but in the name of bamboo - Rick was always in a hurry.

They left the cinema before the film started, with Rick in a frenzy and Sock Sloth feeling a growing sense of dread.

Across the other side of the city, Wacky Bottomsmirk was enjoying his newfound freedom, having smashed his way out of the high-security prison where he'd been kept.

He'd headed straight to The Altar of Power, which is where the true magnificence of the Lunar Blades could be unlocked.

Standing before the altar, Wacky held the two katanas aloft and with a piercing laugh that would strike fear into the bravest of creatures, he began powering up the two blades – his two large tusks bristling with excitement. The more power that surged through the blades, the louder, more insane his laugh became. He loved how they were making him feel. Invincible.

No sloth nor panda were going to stand in his way, to become the most powerful creature of all time.

Everyone in Aridonia would bow in his presence and everyone would grow up knowing his name.

Once the blades were fully charged and the power from them had surged through his considerable bulky brown body and added yet more capability to his already multi-functional cybernetic bodysuit, Wacky smiled menacingly.

He was now ready to unleash his evil plan not only on the city, but once he'd seized control of that, he'd stop at nothing. Nowhere on earth would be safe from Whacky Bottomsmirk – the greatest, most powerful villain of all time.

At least that's what he thought.

CHAPTER 8
THE SOLAR ECLIPSE

The streets of Aridonia were peaceful and calm. The sun was shining brightly, and the warm September air released a fresh but welcome breeze. The birds were singing, and people were working in their everyday offices, doing their everyday jobs, going about their everyday lives. In fact, you could say this was just another normal day.

Except it wasn't.

In a flash, everything changed. A blazing ring of fire spontaneously surrounded the moon, engulfing it in complete darkness. Two dazzling blue lights shone out from underneath it. The Lunar Blades.

With power coursing through his flabby body, Whacky cackled to himself, "Wahaa haaa goodbye Aridonia City!"

Sock Sloth and Rick the Panda turned the corner of the main street in the city to see and hear the sight of Wacky Bottomsmirk taking his revenge.

"Well, it looks like Whacky's gone mad!" chirped Sock Sloth, his voice box feeling unusually tight through fear.

Wacky stopped what he was about to do, his attention now turned to the two super detectives in front of him.

"Mad, am I?" He cackled.

"Yes, you are!" Rick raised his voice loudly. "You're certifiable – you big bamboo binning fiend!"

"Oh yes! Who loves their bamboo so much they'd do anything for it?" Whacky quipped back.

Whilst Rick and Whacky were concentrating on slinging insults at each other, Sock Sloth was trying to spot where the power down button was on Whacky's cybernetic suit. If he could just find that – they might just stand a chance to come out of this alive.

But he was having a hard time doing so.

And amid everything Rick had decided in his wisdom to now run (well it was more of a fast-paced trot) down the road, leaving Sock Sloth at a loss as to where he had gone.

CHAPTER 9
GRANDPA PANDA TO THE RESCUE

Rick knew he had to get help and fast. Except pandas don't really move at speed.

So, he punched in the secret code 226266 on his mobile phone, saying "I'm in a bamboo fix!" in a panicked tone.

No sooner had he put his mobile back into his back-pack, Grandpa Panda came to the rescue on a Harley Davison motorbike, complete with an extra wide sidecar - its engine roaring to a halt next to Rick.

There was no time to lose.

They sped back to where Sock Sloth was. After using his super speed to try and locate the power down switch on Wacky's suit, he was standing feeling dazed and confused. He stood for a moment defenseless, not knowing what to do. As he did so, Rick lassoed him with the length of super strength rope from his backpack, scooping him up into the side car and they hurtled off at speed to the city's military base.

When they arrived with a screech of brakes at the heavily fortified barracks, they were met with a scene they weren't expecting.

The soldiers seemed to be more singsong than getting ready to go to war.

"Hello," said a gruff but authoritarian voice over the intercom. "I'm General RPG – Rocket Pig Grenade in case you don't already know." General RPG then broke into song, RPG – yeah Rocket Pig Grenade, ooh yeah!"

Rick and Sock Sloth stared back blankly at the keypad. Sock Sloth buried his head in his front paw, a sense of dismay filling his socks.

And there they were hoping that the might of the military might save them.

Well, at least they thought it could until they'd been confronted by a warbling pig known as General RPG - who continued to warble when the heroes arrived.

Rick was the first to crack, "Please stop singing!" Rick implored General RPG. "The whole of Aridonia is about to be flattened by an out-of-control power-hungry walrus!"

The singing stopped abruptly.

"Well, why didn't you say so?" General RPG rallied the troops.

Back in Aridonia city, Whacky had been left wondering where Sock Sloth and Rick had gone. One minute they were there, Rick hurling insults, the next a blur of speedy greyish brown fur had been circling him. Then there was a loud roar from a motorbike engine, and then nothing. It's like they had just disappeared into thin air.

Little did Whacky know that Grandpa Panda had deftly delivered Sock Sloth and Rick to General RPG who was now busy overseeing Aridonia's military response to Whacky's antics.

On the back of an armoured truck now stood the largest, most imposing rocket missile Sock Sloth had ever seen. The Boom Boomatron 5000!

It was so powerful it had never been used in open combat – only in one test operation, which had flattened a huge two-mile radius in the depths of the desert – safely away from any living soul.

Now it stood proudly pointing aloft to the sky – its dark blue metal casing shining in the tinges of what now remained of the moonlight.

This time when the troops began to sing again, Sock Sloth and Rick could see it was more of a rallying cry to war. They seemed to be warbling this time about the fear of the Big One. The boys were not sure if they had misheard their intentions as if they were to use the Boom Boomatron 5000, surely it would flatten Aridonia for good.

But apparently not - as General RPG and the troops loaded themselves into vehicles – the second one carrying the huge missile war head in the back.

"Woah!" Sock Sloth countered.

"Well, at least they're taking the threat seriously this time," Rick responded.

"Yes, but we'll be saying goodbye to Aridonia if they use it!" warned Sock Sloth.

CHAPTER 10
WACKY'S WRATH

By the time the army rolled onto the city's streets, Aridonia was all but deserted. Everyone was either cowering under desks or in specially built shelters underground in their homes that had been built for protection.

Whacky was now using the full force of the Lunar Blades and summoning meteors out of the sky to destroy the city. Each crash and explosion seemed louder and more impactful than the last.

Large forks of lightning hurtled down from the heavens and great swarms of armoured iguanas flooded the streets. Aridonia was now unrecognisable.

Wacky continued with his evil plan – summoning creatures lost in times long ago, sinking the desert beneath their feet and orchestrating the descent of Mount Mammoth into the molten depths of a volcano, which rose into the now darkened sky.

The Chillbone Maze was destroyed as it too was swept into the boiling magma, which in turn started to flood the city, leaving a trail of fiery red and orange debris and destruction in its path.

Sock Sloth and Rick the Panda looked on in horror.

Was there no stopping Whacky and his evil plan?

Standing next to them, horrified by the destruction that had been unleashed in her father's name, was Tibono the Blade Keeper – the immortal daughter of The Lunar King. Firmly clasped in her hand was the Spear of Destiny, its ruby red crystal spike faintly glowing on top.

Another meteorite flattened an area – just five streets away from where they stood.

"The meteorites!" shouted Rick as they saw another one hurtling from the sky flattening a large area of land.

"I think that might have been our office you know," said Sock Sloth sadly. "I'll miss that branch!"

"My collection of bamboo!" wailed Rick, as he finally understood the seriousness of what had just happened and how close they were to peril.

Wacky had a crazed stare consuming his face as he summoned humungous Flame Wings, swift Speed Killers, roaring annihilators, and a large imposing scarlet hydra – all intent on as much destruction as possible.

Wacky himself was flying a hundred metres in the sky above, inside a specially built Universal Apocalyptic Mech (UAM) – he had clearly built for this very occasion.

"Wacky's been busy!" Sock Sloth gasped as the hydra's tail narrowly swished past him and Rick at breakneck speed, flattening the local coffee shop and Post Office as it did so.

But the only one who wasn't phased was General RPG. He stood tall and proud from his vehicle – brandishing a loud hailer.

"Whacky Bottomsmirk!" he warned, his deep voice booming and reverberating off the glass shattered surrounding buildings.

For a moment there was silence.

Such was the command that General RPG's voice carried.

"Enough is enough!" General RPG continued.

"If you don't stop – we will have no choice but to launch the Boom Boomatron 5000 on you and your entire evil army."

Sock Sloth and Rick searched for cover – anything that could protect them from such an enormous blast. They were lucky in that instant to spot a now revealed trap door in the middle of the street that led to one of the city's ancient bomb shelters. They motioned for the Blade Keeper to follow them, and they climbed gently inside – hoping to avoid the evil gaze of Whacky as they did.

CHAPTER 11

ROCKET PIG GRENADE

General RPG stood unperturbed by Whacky and his antics. He'd seen it all before. Evil villains that wanted to take over the world for their own gain. But none had gotten the better of him yet and he resolved that Wacky certainly wouldn't do so now.

"Whacky Bottomsmirk," he commanded through his loud hailer – "This," he motioned to the giant missile beside him, "is the Boom Boomatron 5000 – the most powerful weapon known – and it's heading your way unless you stop this madness."

For the first time, Wacky felt a strange sensation coursing through his brown blubby body. Could it be fear?

"I, I'd rather you didn't" he conceded.

"Launch it anyway and then invoke escape plan A," General RPG commanded his lieutenant who nodded in response before radioing the rest of the army, so they knew exactly what to do next. They would only have 20 seconds to escape the carnage and stay safe.

And then it dawned on Wacky that it was he who should be in control as he had the Lunar Blades.

"But General you forget," Wacky said slyly, "I still have these," wielding the Lunar Blades aloft he started to cackle, all whilst encased in his Universal Apocalyptic Mech.

But General RPG was in no mood for negotiations.

As the Boom Boomatron 5000 hurtled towards Wacky with little to no warning, Wacky was caught off guard. Panicking, he leapt out of his UAM, brandishing the Lunar Blades.

The Boom Boomatron 5000 was quick to respond and changed course to follow Wacky, much to his surprise.

In the same moment, General RPG unnoticed by anyone, launched himself into the air, crept inside Wacky's now disguarded UAM. On entering, he pressed the ultra-defense mode button, Wacky had failed to notice, and used it to fire a rocket at him.

The rocket immediately hit Wacky in the head knocking him even more off guard.

"Rocket!" the General announced. "Pig" he shouted. Then he threw a highly toxic one-of-a-kind grenade that worked in conjunction with the Boom Boomatron 5000 from the UAM "Grenade"!

This all happened in the space of 15 seconds. And in the next five seconds - the skies above Aridonia were lit up in the brightest, most startling light ever seen as an almighty shockwave was felt by everyone within a two-mile radius. The Boom Boomatron 5000 had exploded.

After the smoke had cleared, and everything was eerily quiet, Sock Sloth peered out from beneath the trap door where they had safely survived the enormous blast.

Wacky Bottomsmirk had been thrown to the ground and his cybernetic suit was fizzing with smoke. "I still have the Lunar Blades you know," he gasped.

"Oh no you don't!" bellowed the Blade Keeper and as she held aloft the Spear of Destiny, the blades returned to her, before she disappeared into what looked like thin air.

General RPG's carefully crafted Plan A meant that the army had escaped onto a nearby aircraft carrier, which was now about to launch out to sea.

He bundled a weary Whacky Bottomsmirk, Sock Sloth and Rick the Panda into the UAM and flew them to the aircraft carrier for safety.

But on landing, something happened that none of them could have foreseen.

CHAPTER 12

A WATERY SURPRISE

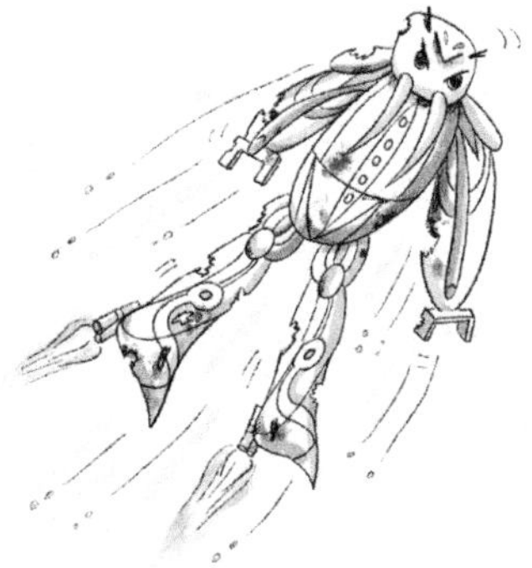

Without the Lunar Blades, Wacky may have been weakened, but he was still intent on wreaking havoc.

And he had one more surprise concealed in his fizzing cybernetic suit. He could still fly!

It might not have been as fast or as powerful now he no longer had the Lunar Blades, but he certainly wasn't going to become a prisoner of the military. And he certainly wasn't going to be taken down by that sloth and panda from that Super Awesome Dude crime fighting agency.

As General RPG commanded his team to take Wacky below deck to the prison cells on board, Wacky pressed the button that would enable him to fly. The metallic boots on his suit transformed into flaming rockets as he shot into the sky.

His whiskers bristled with joy – he'd fooled them all again and had lived to see another day.

No matter that his iguana army had been wiped out by that Boom Boomatron blast or that the other creatures he'd summoned had met with an untimely end as a result. As long as he was ok that was all that mattered.

But no one could have imagined what happened next.

The waves of the ocean roared, and the aircraft carrier shook violently to one side.

In the commotion, Rick had to grab not only Sock Sloth's paw, but also his backpack as it started to slide out of reach. Thankfully, it was saved by the quick thinking of Grandpa Panda and his left foot, which was outstretched for any such eventualities.

A large purple tentacle slammed the ship sideways into a giant wave.

Even General RPG looked on in awe at what was unfolding in front of them.

Wacky was so busy congratulating himself on yet another marvellous escape that he failed to realise the enormity of the Eliminator Kraken that was rising out of the ocean towards him.

With its seven huge, shiny tentacles outstretched towards him, Whacky was soon being guided into its large, fanged mouth.

As everyone on the aircraft carrier looked on in horror, Wacky Bottomsmirk had been swallowed whole, before the kraken retreated to the ocean bed below – having had its first, and quite substantial meal of the day.

CHAPTER 13

THE RETURN OF THE LUNAR KING

No sooner had the Eliminator Kraken disappeared into the depths of the water below, than a beam of bright blue light shone down onto the deck of the aircraft carrier.

Emerging from that bright blue light was the tall, imposing figure of a man wearing bright blue robes and a sparkling dark blue crown to match.

Sock Sloth and Rick the Panda gasped in unison.

When they'd first been called upon to help with the case of the missing Lunar Blades – this was the exact image

Sock Sloth had seen in the book that helped them with their research. This was the Lunar King himself!

Emerging from the light to stand next to her father stood Tibono, the Blade Keeper.

The man's wisened face shone down on them.

"Thank you!" he began, his grand voice reverberating through them all.

"I am Nikara, The Lunar King and I've seen what happens when these blades are in the wrong hands. Wacky Bottomsmirk could have destroyed entire galaxies. I am beyond grateful to you all for helping my daughter stay safe and for ensuring that I now have these once more albeit in a different and safer dimension."

"Although Aridonia will still need some rebuilding," Tibono continued, "We have used the power of the blades to ensure everyone still there, is safe. But of course, there will never be another Chillbone Maze."

Then turning to Sock Sloth and Rick the Panda, she continued, "Aridonia is lucky to have heroes like you who help when no one else does."

The Lunar King nodded in General RPG's direction. "Your bravery has not gone unnoticed."

And with that The Lunar King and his daughter disappeared into thin air, but not before a flick of the blades, where a corner of the ship was transformed into a mountain of freshly growing bamboo shoots and a branch or two – just right for a special sloth to hang upside down when he wanted.

There was a hushed silence on board the ship as everyone digested what had just happened.

In between it all, Rick and Grandpa Panda's tummies rumbled.

"Well, if this isn't time for bamboo then I don't know when is!" chuckled Grandpa Panda.

Sock Sloth and Rick looked at each other and smiled.

"A new adventure into the unknown," said Sock Sloth.

"With you all the way," smiled Rick.

The two friends were on a voyage with the best of company, and a lot of singsong, courtesy of their military friends.

THE END

About the Author

J W B Rowley is nine.

Alongside writing stories, he loves to build worlds on Minecraft, is an aspiring actor, and keen swimmer and cricketer.

Sock Sloth and the Lunar Blades is his debut book.

With a love for all things panda and sloth related, he was inspired to come up with this story during a visit to Edinburgh Zoo, after seeing the pandas before they returned to China.

You can find out more about J as one of our child authors at Rainbow House Publishing - www.rainbowhousepublishing.com

Printed in Great Britain
by Amazon

44357615R00030